The Scotsman Guide to Scottish Politics

£3

D0492421